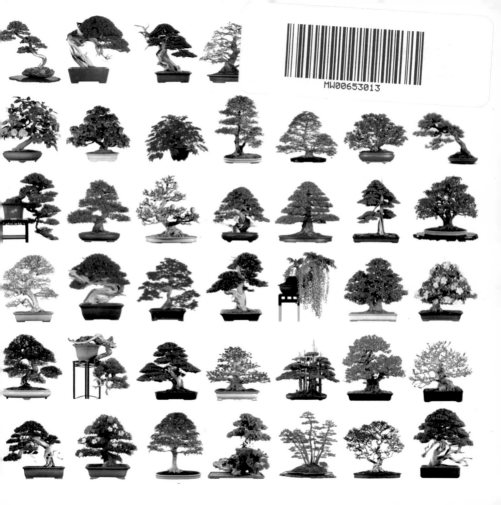

MW00653013

Published in the United States of America in 2008 by
Stone Lantern Publishing
A Division of Stone Lantern Discoveries, Inc.
125 Meeting House Hill
Passumpsic, VT 05861

Copyright 2008 by Stone Lantern Publishing.

Designed by Joseph Schoech.

All rights reserved. No part of this publication may be
reproduced in any manner whatsoever without
permission in writing from Stone Lantern Publishing.

ISBN 978-0-9767550-5-0
LC 2007909267

Printed and bound in China.

Preface

There are only a few things you need to make good bonsai: good plant material, good tools, good technique and great examples. The great examples serve to inspire and to instruct and are what this book is about.

The inspiration comes when you first see the trees. The instruction comes when you carefully study what the masters have done. When you combine inspiration and instruction, your enjoyment of bonsai will increase dramatically. So will the beauty of your trees.

This book was conceived of, compiled and designed by Joseph Schoech. All the photos are from the covers of Bonsai Today magazine, issues 1-99.

We hope that you enjoy this small offering and that you find it inspirational and instructive.

Yours in beautiful and healthy bonsai,

Wayne Schoech

Editor & Publisher
Stone Lantern Publishing
November 22, 2007

CHINESE QUINCE *PSOCYDONIA SINENSIS* 1

2 JAPANESE WHITE PINE *PINUS PARVIFLORA*

SHIMPAKU JUNIPER *JUNIPERUS CHINENSIS* 3

4 SHIMPAKU JUNIPER *JUNIPERUS CHINENSIS*

JAPANESE MAPLE *ACER PALMATUM ATROPURPUREUM* 5

6 JAPANESE HAWTHORN *CRATAEGUS CUNEATA*

JAPANESE BLACK PINE *PINUS THUNBERGII* 7

8 KAMATSUKA *PHOTINIA VILLOSA*

NEEDLE JUNIPER *JUNIPERUS RIGIDA* 9

10 FULLMOON MAPLE *ACER JAPONICUM*

12 JAPANESE WHITE PINE *PINUS PARVIFLORA*

STEWARTIA *STEWARTIA MONADELPHA* 13

14 JAPANESE WINTERBERRY *ILEX SERRATA*

SHIMPAKU JUNIPER *JUNIPERUS CHINENSIS* 15

16 FIRETHORN *PYRACANTHA 'DUVALII'*

JAPANESE FLOWERING APRICOT *PRUNUS MUME* 17

18 CHINESE QUINCE *PSEUDOCYDONIA SINENSIS*

JAPANESE MAPLE *ACER PALMATUM* 19

20 EZO SPRUCE *PICEA GLEHNII*

JAPANESE BLACK PINE *PINUS THUNBERGII* 21

22 JAPANESE MAPLE *ACER PALMATUM*

JAPANESE BLACK PINE *PINUS THUNBERGII* 23

24 NEEDLE JUNIPER *JUNIPERUS RIGIDA*

JAPANESE WHITE PINE *PINUS PARVIFLORA* 25

26 GRAY BARK ELM *ZELKOVA SERRATA*

JAPANESE WHITE PINE *PINUS PARVIFLORA* 27

28 EZO SPRUCE *PICEA GLEHNII*

SCARLET KADSURA *KADSURA JAPONICA* 29

30 SATSUKI AZALEA *RHODODENDRON INDICUM*

JAPANESE BLACK PINE *PINUS THUNBERGII* 31

32 SATSUKI AZALEA *RHODODENDRON INDICLIM*

SHIMPAKU JUNIPER *JUNIPERUS CHINENSIS* 33

34 SATSUKI AZALEA *RHODODENDRON INDICUM*

36 ENGLISH HAWTHORN *CRATAEGUS LAEVIGATA*

38 JAPANESE RED PINE *PINUS DENSIFLORA*

THREAD LEAF JAPANESE MAPLE *ACER PALAMATUM DISSECTUM* 39

40 VIBURNUM *VIBURNUM DILATUM*

BOSTON IVY *PARTHENOCISSUS TRICUSPIDATA* 41

42 JAPANESE WHITE PINE *PINUS PARVIFLORA*

JAPANESE WHITE *PINE PINUS PARVIFLORA* 43

44 JAPANESE YEW *TAXUS CUSPIDATA*

GRAY-BARK ELM *ZELKOVA SERRATA* 45

46 CHINESE QUINCE *PSEUDOCYDONIA SINENSIS*

48 FLOWERING PLUM *PRUNUS SALICINA*

JAPANESE WHITE PINE *PINUS PARVIFLORA* 49

50 JAPANESE BLACK PINE *PINUS THUNBERGII*

SATSUKI AZALEA *RHODODENDRON INDICUM* 51

52 JAPANESE WISTERIA *WISTERIA FLORIBUNDA*

54 CHINESE QUINCE *PSEUDOCYDONIA SINENSIS*

ROCK HORNBEAM *CARPINUS TURCZANINO* 55

56 JAPANESE WHITE PINE *PINUS PARVIFLORA*

58 JAPANESE YEW *TAXUS CUSPIDATA*

FUJI FLOWERING CHERRY *PRUNUS INCISA* 59

60 JAPANESE WINTERBERRY *ILEX SERRATA*

EZO SPRUCE *PICEA GLEHNII* 61

62 CHINESE QUINCE *PSEUDOCYDONIA SINENSIS*

64 JAPANESE BLACK PINE *PINUS THUNBERGII*

SATSUKI AZALEA *RHODODENDRON INDICUM* 65

66 CAMELLIA *CAMELLIA SASANQUA*

LINDEN VIBURNUM *VIBURNUM DILATATUM* 67

68 BOSTON IVY *PARTHENOCISSUS TRICUSPIDATA*

POMEGRANATE *PUNICA GRANATUM* 69

70 JAPANESE MAPLE *ACER PALMATUM*

DWARF CRABAPPLE *MALUS MICROMALUS* 71

72 TAMARISK *TAMARIX JUNIPERINA*

JAPANESE WHITE PINE *PINUS PARVIFLORA* 73

74 JAPANESE ZELKOVA *ZELKOVA SERRATA*

NEEDLE JUNIPER *JUNIPERUS RIGIDA* 75

76 JAPANESE BLACK PINE *PINUS THUNBERGII*

78 CHINESE QUINCE *PSEUDOCYDONIA SINENSIS*

80 JAPANESE WHITE PINE *PINUS PARVIFLORA*

NEEDLE JUNIPER *JUNIPERUS RIGIDA* 81

82 CHINESE QUINCE *PSEUDOCYDONIA SINESIS*

84 JAPANESE MAPLE *ACER PALMATUM DISSECTUM*

JAPANESE BLACK *PINE PINUS THUNBERGII* 85

86 KOREAN HORNBEAM *CARPINUS TURCZANINOVI*

88 JAPANESE MAPLE *ACER PALMATUM DISSECTUM*

90 JAPANESE WISTERIA *WISTERIA FLORIBUNDA*

92 SATSUKI AZALEA *RHODODENDRON INDICUM*

94 JAPANESE FLOWERING APRICOT *PRUNUS MUME*

96 TEA TREE *LEPTOSPERMUM SCOPARIUM*

98 NEEDLE JUNIPER *JUNIPERUS RIGIDA*

Get Back Issues of
Bonsai Today
While They Last

**By the year - 2000 - 2006
available - 6 issues $55 USA,
$70 elsewhere shipping included**

Individual Issues **26 - 108** most still
available **$12.00** each

FREE shipping for quantities

stonelantern.com

Majesty in Miniature
Shohin Bonsai
Unlocking the Secrets
of Small Trees

by Morten Albek
with Wayne Schoech

Shohin bonsai cost less (pot and tree), take less time to develop, take less space, are easier to move, are less apt to be overwatered, and, are delight to behold.

This detailed, thorough and beautiful exploration of the art of small bonsai is geared for experienced bonsai enthusiasts and daring beginners. If you already appreciate and practice the art, Shohin Bonsai will deepen your understanding. If you don't, now is the time to unlock the secrets of small trees.

Morten Albek has been practicing and teaching Shohin bonsai in Europe for years. In addition to being an accomplished Shohin artist and expert on the various facets of Shohin bonsai, Morten is a masterful photographer - as the exquisite photos in this benchmark book will attest.

Softcover. 7.5" x 9.5"
198 pages
B1SHOHIN $24.95

Satsuki Azaleas
for bonsai & azalea enthusiasts

This remarkable book by Robert Callaham presents by far the most expert, detailed information on Satsuki bonsai of any English language book. It is hard to imagine that we will ever need another book on the subject. If you haven't had the pleasure of growing Satsuki bonsai, don't wait. They are as brilliant and beautiful as any plant on earth. And they take to bonsai culture like fish to water.

Rich with photographs, how-to instructions, fascinating facts, and an unrivaled encyclopedia of over 1,600 cultivars (this alone is worth the book's price). All of this adds up to a rare treasure indeed.

Softcover. 10 3/4" x 8 3/4" 240 pages, full of dramatic color photos
B1SAT $39.95

Bonsai from the Wild

Nick Lenz's classic book is back in print and is a must for any serious bonsai enthusiast. Completely revised, expanded and redesigned—with 90 more pages and numerous new color photos. An amazing collection of valuable information for anyone interested in bonsai.

Nick is one of North America's best known bonsai artists and for good reason. His breadth and depth of knowledge and artistry places him among the world's greatest experts. If you want to learn about collecting, or really almost anything about bonsai art and horticulture, this book is essential.

Softcover. 10 3/4" x 8 3/4" 192 pages, 200+ color photos
B1LENZ $29.95

Bonsai Today Masters Series

Pines

Growing & Styling Japanese Black & White Pines

Without understanding the challenges and subtleties involved, it is impossible to style and maintain beautiful pine bonsai. This definitive book is designed to help you understand and master those challenges. And of course, to enjoy the majestic beauty of some of nature's finest trees.

Includes: galleries, needle reduction and energy balancing (candle pinching, shoot pruning, needle plucking and bud removal), styles and styling, nebari development, branch development, sacrifice branches, branch bending, shari and jin, rock plantings, transplanting, choosing a pot, plant positioning, growing from seed, care, maintenance, superfeeding, winter-care and much more.

Softcover. 8 1/2 x 11"
184 pages. 300 color photos.
B1PINES $29.95

800.776.1167
stonelantern.com

Bonsai Today Masters Series
Junipers
Growing & Styling Juniper Bonsai

BONSAI TODAY MASTERS' SERIES
JUNIPERS

GROWING & STYLING JUNIPER BONSAI
SHIMPAKU, NEEDLE, PROCUMBENS, CALIFORNIA AND OTHER JUNIPERS
COMPILED & EDITED BY WAYNE SCHOECH & THE STAFF OF BONSAI TODAY

This magnificent book brings together, for the first time, wisdom and experience gathered from around the globe in one comprehensive reference work. Here you can learn from the masters, from generations of experience. You can unearth secrets, gain ideas and inspiration, and learn techniques that you may never have imagined. After reading this book, you will approach your juniper bonsai with a new understanding and increased confidence. You will find more satisfaction in your work and, more important, you will gain increased joy when you contemplate the fruits of your labor.
- From the foreword by Colin Lewis

The definitive book on junipers. Learn a range of techniques and tips from the masters—Masahiko Kimura, Noboru Kaneko, Kunio Kobayashi, Harry Hirao, Tomio Yamada, Shinji Suzuki, and others. Varieties featured are: Shimpaku, Needle juniper, Procumbens juniper, California juniper and more. The techniques featured are applicable across the range of junipers. This unique book also features a wonderful gallery of bonsai by great Japanese masters and prominent Westerners like John Naka, Boon Manakitivipart, Ernie Kuo and others. In addition to all this, there is an introduction to junipers featuring a species guide and a chapter on juniper care and maintenance. You and your bonsai will enjoy and benefit from this new benchmark book.

Softcover. 8 1/2" x 11" 184 pages.
B1JUN $29.95